Table of Contents

DEDICATION

To all my past, present, and future students.
Stay focussed till you achieve your academic dreams.

PREFACE

Greetings!

It gives me great pleasure to introduce this book to all researchers, research students and faculty members. This handbook will be a good guide to those who are embarking on a research journey as a student, be it at the doctoral or master's degree levels.

This handbook is designed to be a light reading guide with clear steps to face various situations that might confront a postgraduate research student. Ideas shared here are from the perspective of a practitioner.

 Though this book is targeting postgraduate research students, it does not in any way challenge the need for students to adhere to institutional guidelines and requirements.

I would like to thank my colleagues and postgraduate students who I have supervised and examined over the years for the insights I have shared in this handbook. I would like to acknowledge that my professional practice as a teacher, lecturer, supervisor, and examiner is impacted by the many casual and formal discussions I have had within the classroom and beyond since I started my teaching career in tthhe 80s.

I often share with my colleagues and postgraduate students that embarking on a postgraduate research programme and ensuring successful completion of it is no easy task, especially if you are a working adult, but with the correct guidance, this task is very possible. Hence, the decision to come up with this book for my students and others who are determined to take this academic journey.

23 March 2023

Chapter 1

INTRODUCTION

Welcome to A Handbook for Postgraduate Research Students! This handbook is designed to provide you with a comprehensive guide to navigating the postgraduate research journey. This chapter outlines the purpose and scope of the handbook and provides an overview of what to expect during the postgraduate research journey. The contents of this book are based on my personal experience as a Ph.D. supervisor and my observation of the challenges students face in their journey through their studies. The suggestions I share here are tips that I share with my students as well.

The objective of this handbook is to give you useful guidance, pointers, and resources so you can excel in your postgraduate research studies. This handbook is intended to be a useful tool for you, whether you are just getting started or are already well into your research. It guides you through every step of the demanding and fulfilling process of postgraduate research. The handbook offers guidance on the postgraduate research procedure, aids in the development of the skills and knowledge required for advanced-level research, and supports students in generating a thesis or dissertation of the highest quality.

The scope of this handbook covers a wide range of topics that are essential for postgraduate research students, including choosing a research topic, formulating research questions, conducting literature reviews, collecting and analyzing data, and writing up your findings. It also provides advice on time management, data management, academic writing, networking, and maintaining a healthy work-life balance. This handbook covers designing research methodology and preparing for the viva voce examination. It also offers tips on how to manage the emotional and psychological challenges that can arise during the research journey.

My personal experience as a postgraduate student and my experience of designing and teaching a special course on thesis writing to postgraduate students has also informed the contents of this handbook.

The postgraduate research journey can be a challenging and demanding experience and at the same time a rewarding and intellectually stimulating one. You can expect to encounter many opportunities for growth and learning, as well as some obstacles and setbacks along the way. This handbook will guide you through the various stages of postgraduate research, from the initial planning stages to the final stages of writing up and publishing your research findings. It is designed to be a practical resource that you can refer to throughout your postgraduate research journey, providing guidance and advice on a wide range of topics related to research:

1. Planning and structuring your research project
2. Conducting literature reviews
3. Collecting and analyzing data

4.   Writing and presenting your research

5.   Managing your time effectively

6.   Building relationships with your supervisor
     and other academics

7.   Navigating ethical issues in research

8.   Dealing with stress and managing your
     wellbeing

9.   Preparing for your viva and the final stages
     of your research

This handbook will give you useful guidance, hints, and resources to support your research activities. There will also be general discussions on the opinions and experiences of academics, researchers, and other postgraduate research students.

The journey through the postgraduate exams can be demanding and challenging, but it can also be rewarding and psychologically stimulating. Many opportunities for growth and learning will present themselves to you, along with some stumbling blocks and unfortunate events. Take every incident as a challenge that every postgraduate will have to endure to achieve their dreams. This guide will walk you through each step of the postgraduate examination process, from the preliminary planning stages to the final steps of reviewing and disseminating your research findings.

I hope that this handbook will help you to achieve your goals and reach your full potential as a postgraduate research student. Remember, you are not alone on this journey, and there is support available to help you along the way. Reach out to your family, friends, peers, and your supervisory committee for support. Good luck!

NOTES

Chapter 2

GETTING STARTED

Selecting a research topic at the postgraduate level can be challenging, but it is essential to choose a topic that aligns with your interests, skills, and career aspirations. The topic you choose would be your passion for at least 3 years of your life and you need to sustain your interest and energy till you complete your studies.

Here are some tips to help you select a research topic:

a. **Start by identifying your research interests:** Think about the topics that excite you and the areas where you have some prior knowledge or expertise.

A good starting point will be your undergraduate research projects or your Master's degree dissertation. At the doctoral level, you can expand the topics you explored in your earlier research projects.

Most doctoral students select topics that are related to their jobs e.g. teaching and learning, administration, and leadership. However, remember that whatever topic selected must be current and relevant to the present situation.

Below are examples of research topics in different areas of study:

Language

1. With the increasing availability and accessibility of technology, researchers are investigating the effectiveness of using technology in language learning, such as online language courses, language learning apps, and virtual reality simulations.
2. Research is being conducted on effective strategies for teacher education and professional development in language teaching, such as training in second language acquisition theories

and teaching techniques, and the use of reflective practice.

3. Research on the implications of multilingualism and language policy in education, such as the role of the home language in academic achievement and the impact of language policies on language learning and teaching is also trending.

4. The use of language in real-world tasks and activities, rather than isolated language practice, and the effectiveness of this approach in language teaching and learning, is another current research topic.

5. Researchers are investigating the role of learner autonomy and self-regulated learning in language learning, such as the development of metacognitive strategies, motivation, and self-efficacy.

6. Language learning with subject matter content, such as science, math, or social studies, and the effectiveness of this approach in promoting language proficiency and content knowledge is popular as well.

7. Research on effective language assessment, such as the use of performance-based assessments,

formative assessments, and the use of technology in assessment is gaining traction as well.

Environment

1. Climate change has been trending for several years and continues to be a top priority for environmental research. Climate change research focuses on understanding the causes, impacts, and potential solutions to the changing climate, including the role of greenhouse gas emissions, deforestation, and adaptation measures.

2. The loss of biodiversity is a critical environmental issue, and research in this area aims to understand the impacts of human activities on ecosystems and the conservation strategies needed to protect biodiversity.

3. Sustainable development research focuses on balancing economic, social, and environmental considerations in the pursuit of long-term development goals. This includes research on sustainable agriculture, renewable energy, and green infrastructure.

4. Research in environmental health focuses on the relationship between environmental factors and

human health. This includes research on air and water pollution, exposure to toxins, and the health impacts of climate change.

5. Environmental justice research focuses on the unequal distribution of environmental risks and benefits among different communities. This includes research on the disproportionate impacts of pollution and climate change on marginalized communities and the development of policies to address these disparities.

6. The circular economy is an economic model that aims to reduce waste and promote resource efficiency. Research in this area focuses on understanding the environmental and economic benefits

Artificial Intelligence

1. Natural Language Processing (NLP) is an area of AI that focuses on developing algorithms and models to understand and generate human language. Research in this field can involve developing better machine translation systems, sentiment analysis, or text summarization.

2. Machine Learning (ML) involves developing algorithms that enable machines to learn and make predictions based on data. Research in this field can involve developing more accurate models or creating new approaches to data pre-processing and feature extraction.

3. Computer Vision (CV) is an area of AI that focuses on developing algorithms to enable machines to "see" and interpret visual data. Research in this field can involve developing better object recognition systems, image segmentation, or video analysis.

4. Robotics involves designing and developing machines that can interact with the physical world. Research in this field can involve developing new robotic systems, improving robotic perception and control, or creating new applications for robots.

5. Human-Computer Interaction (HCI) is an interdisciplinary field that focuses on the design and evaluation of computer systems that are easy and efficient to use. Research in this field can involve developing new user interfaces,

evaluating the usability of existing systems, or studying how people interact with technology.

6. Cybersecurity is an increasingly important field that focuses on protecting computer systems and networks from unauthorized access, attacks, and damage. Research in this field can involve developing new encryption algorithms, designing secure systems, or developing better intrusion detection and prevention systems.

7. Data science involves using statistical and computational methods to analyze and extract insights from large datasets. Research in this field can involve developing new algorithms or models for data analysis, creating new techniques for data visualization, or developing new approaches to data storage and management.

Media and Communication

1. Social media and its impact on society, politics, and communication

2. Fake news, misinformation, and disinformation in the media

3. The role of media in shaping public opinion and attitudes

4. Media and technology convergence, including topics such as mobile media, virtual reality, and augmented reality

5. Media literacy, including education, awareness, and critical thinking skills for media users

6. Media diversity and representation, including issues of gender, race, ethnicity, and sexual orientation

7. Journalism ethics and professionalism, including issues of objectivity, accountability, and transparency

8. Media effects on health and well-being, including topics such as media violence, body image, and mental health

9. The economics of media, including issues of ownership, advertising, and revenue models

10. Media regulation and policy, including topics such as censorship, media ownership, and the impact of government policy on the media industry.

Engineering

1. There is a growing interest in renewable energy sources such as solar, wind, hydro, and

geothermal energy, as well as energy storage and efficiency.

2. Artificial Intelligence and the use of machine learning, computer vision, and natural language processing is growing in fields such as robotics, autonomous vehicles, and smart cities.

3. Internet of Things (IoT) which relates to the interconnectivity of devices, sensors, and networks is enabling the creation of smart homes, factories, and cities, as well as improving healthcare and transportation.

4. Developments in biomedical engineering, biomaterials, medical imaging, and drug delivery systems are improving healthcare and medical treatments.

5. With the increasing reliance on technology, cybersecurity is becoming more critical than ever to protect sensitive data and infrastructure.

6. Advanced materials such as graphene, carbon nanotubes, and metamaterials are being developed for their unique properties and potential applications in electronics, energy storage, and aerospace.

7. The development of autonomous systems, such as drones and self-driving cars, is accelerating, leading to new challenges and opportunities.

8. The next generation of wireless networks is expected to revolutionize communication and enable new applications in areas such as virtual and augmented reality, gaming, and smart cities.

9. The use of robots is increasing in fields such as manufacturing, healthcare, and exploration.

10. Virtual and augmented reality are technologies that are being used in fields such as education, entertainment, and healthcare to enhance the user experience and enable new forms of interaction.

Information Technology

1. Artificial Intelligence (AI) and Machine Learning (ML) are the most significant trend in information technology currently. Research in this area focuses on developing new algorithms, techniques, and applications of AI and ML in various fields.

2. With the increase in cyber threats and data breaches, research in cybersecurity is becoming more important. This includes topics such as cryptography, network security, and security protocols.

3. Cloud computing has become a popular method for delivering computing services over the internet. Research in this area is focused on improving the performance, security, and scalability of cloud-based systems.

4. Big data and analytics relate to the amount of data generated every day which is increasing rapidly, and research in this area focuses on developing new methods and tools for analyzing and processing large datasets.

5. Internet of Things (IoT) refers to the connection of physical devices and objects to the internet. Research in this area focuses on developing new technologies, protocols, and standards for IoT devices.

6. Blockchain research is exploring new use cases for distributed ledger technology beyond cryptocurrencies, such as supply chain

management, voting systems, and digital identity verification.

b. **Conduct a literature review**: Look for gaps or areas that require further research in your field of interest. This will give you an idea of what has been done and what needs to be done.

Conducting a literature review is an essential part of any research project, and it can help you identify gaps or areas that require further research in your field of interest. Conducting a literature review is an essential step in any research project. It allows you to identify existing knowledge, gaps, and areas for further investigation in your field of interest.

Do not be overwhelmed by the amount of reading you will need to do at the postgraduate level. Learn strategies for speed reading such as skimming and scanning. These reading skills will guide you to reading extensively within a short period of time. Here are the steps to conduct a literature review and look for gaps. As you start reading, try to grasp the topic that interests you as this will narrow your search for related literature. This will also help you focus on your research question. You need to have a clear research question in mind before starting your literature review. This will help you focus your search and identify relevant literature.

Start by searching for relevant literature using academic databases, such as Google Scholar, Web of Science, Connected Papers, ResearchGate, Mendeley, or PubMed. Use keywords related to your research question to identify relevant articles, books, and other sources. Check digital databases available in your university and even public libraries.

Once you have identified relevant literature, you need to evaluate it to determine its quality and relevance to your research question. Look for articles that have been published in peer-reviewed journals, and assess the methodology, results, and conclusions of each article. Maintaining a research matrix to keep a record of all the materials you read is a good practice. A sample research matrix is available at the end of this book (Appendix A). This will also ensure that you have sufficient related literature for your thesis.

Maintaining the research matrix will guide you to conducting critical analysis and synthesis of materials you read. As you read the literature, identify themes and patterns that emerge. Look for areas where there is a consensus or disagreement among researchers, and identify any gaps in the literature.

Once you have identified themes and gaps, you need to synthesize the literature to draw conclusions about what is known and what is not known in your field of interest. This can help you identify areas where further research is needed.

Finally, write your literature review, summarizing the key themes, findings, and gaps in the literature. Be sure to provide a critical analysis of the literature and highlight areas where further research is needed. To write a critical analysis, use a Venn diagram to analyse similarities and differences in the materials read. My students find this guide extremely useful to analyse related literature in a critical manner.

An example is shown in Diagram 1:

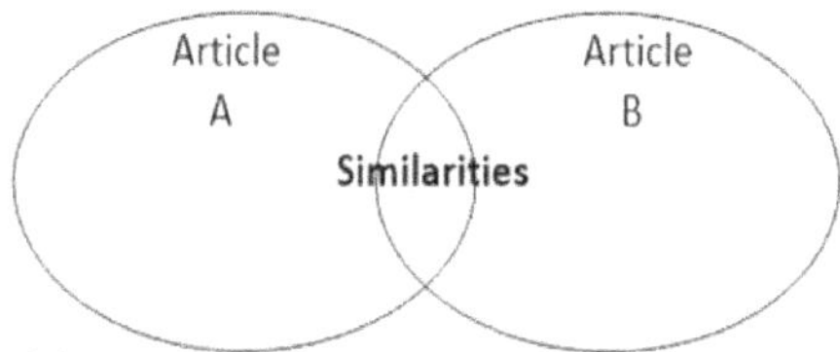

Diagram 1: Analysis of articles

The two articles (A and B) can be analysed using a Venn diagram to identify the similarities and differences in the articles. The intersecting part will be the similarities in the two research. This can be used as a sound basis for writing a critical review of the two articles.

By following these steps, you can conduct a thorough literature review and identify gaps or areas that require further research in your field of interest. Remember to keep your research questions in mind throughout the process and focus on finding literature that is relevant to your specific topic.

c. **Consider the feasibility of the topic:** Ensure that the research questions are manageable in terms of time, resources, and scope.

Considering the feasibility of a topic for postgraduate research is essential to ensure that the research question is manageable in terms of time, resources, and scope.
Here are some steps you can take to evaluate the feasibility of your research topic.

Before deciding on a research topic, it is essential to conduct a comprehensive literature review to understand the current state of research in your field. This will help you identify the research gaps and determine whether your research question is feasible and relevant. Considering the feasibility of a topic for postgraduate research is essential to ensure that the research question is manageable in terms of time, resources, and scope.

Here are some steps you can take to evaluate the feasibility of your research topic:

Once you have identified a research question, you need to define the scope of your research. Determine the research objectives, the research methodology, the data collection and analysis techniques, and the time required to complete your research.

The researcher intentionally defines the scope to set the boundaries and the scope of the study is presented in the first chapter of your thesis or dissertation. This is important as you are informing your examiners/readers the parameters of your research.

Consider the resources required to complete your research, including funding, equipment, data, and personnel. Determine the availability and accessibility of these resources and evaluate whether they are sufficient for your research.

Identify any potential limitations that may affect the feasibility of your research, such as ethical concerns, access to participants or data, or external factors such as the COVID-19 pandemic. Limitations are beyond the researcher's control. Present the limitations of your research in your final chapter as you will be able to identify the limitations of your study only upon completing your research.

Share your research proposal with your supervisor, friends, family, colleagues, or other experts in your field. Seek their feedback and suggestions for improving the feasibility of your research. Always ensure confidentiality of discussions as an interesting research topic can get published before your research is completed.

Create a realistic timeline for the research project, including key milestones and deadlines. Ensure that the timeline is achievable, given your other commitments and the availability of resources. Explore how to use a Gantt chart to set your milestone. Refer to the sample given at the end of this handbook (Appendix B).

Based on your literature review, scope, resource assessment, and feedback refine your research question to ensure that it is manageable and feasible within the timeframe of your study.

Overall, it is essential to evaluate the feasibility of your research topic to ensure that your research question is achievable within the time and resources available. By following the steps outlined above, you can assess the feasibility of your research topic and ensure that your research question is manageable, relevant, and meaningful.

d.   Consult your supervisors: Discuss your research interests and ideas with your supervisors to receive feedback and guidance. Always maintain a healthy professional relationship with your supervisors. Make them your first point of reference when it comes to the technicalities of your postgraduate journey.

Consulting your supervisor is an important step in the research process as it can help you refine your research ideas and ensure that your proposed project aligns with the interests and expertise of your supervisor. However, often, I remind my supervisees that at the Ph.D. level, students must be independent learners and ensure all procedures are checked and followed as required. Do not wait for your supervisor to nudge you every now and then. You must take full control of your own postgraduate journey. The degree earned is meant for you and not for your supervisor. As such, make sure that you are deserving of the postgraduate degree.

Here are some tips on approaching your supervisors to discuss your research interests and ideas. Start by researching the faculty who have expertise in your research area. Look at their publications, research interests, and background to determine if they might be a good fit for your project. Then, prepare a research proposal that outlines your research interests, questions, and proposed methodology. This will help you articulate your ideas and provide a starting point for the conversation.

It is important that you keep in close contact with your supervisor. Send an email to your supervisor introducing yourself, explaining your research interests, and expressing your interest in working with them. Attach your research proposal to the email. Share your proposal with your supervisor early in your journey so that any revisions

Once you receive a response from your supervisor, schedule a meeting to discuss your proposal in more detail. Make sure to provide a few dates and times that work for you and be flexible in case they are not available. Before the meeting, review your proposal and think about any questions or concerns that the supervisor might have about your research area or topic. Be prepared to discuss your research interests and ideas in more detail.

During the meeting, listen carefully to the feedback and guidance provided by your supervisor. It is important that you maintain a journal to keep a record of your meetings and discussions with your supervisor. Remember to record the date and time of the meetings as well.

Take notes and ask follow-up questions to clarify
any points that are unclear.

After the meeting, send a thank-you email to your
supervisor and summarize the key points
discussed during the meeting. This will help
ensure that you are both on the same page and
have a clear understanding of the next steps. It is
important that you keep the supervisor updated
on discussions before the next meeting so that
both of you are clear about what is the agenda for
the next meeting.

Remember that the goal of the meeting is to
receive feedback and guidance on your research
ideas, so be open to suggestions and willing to
make changes to your proposal based on the
feedback provided by your supervisor.

e.   Developing a research proposal

Developing a research proposal is an essential part
of the postgraduate research process. The proposal
should provide a detailed plan of your research

project, including the research objectives and questions, methodology, data collection and analysis techniques, and timeline.

Here are some tips to help you develop a research proposal. Read and follow the guidelines and format provided by your institution for preparing the research proposal. Provide a brief overview of the existing research in your field and explain how your research project will contribute to the field. Describe the research methodology by introducing the research paradigm, research approach, and research design. Describe the data collection techniques you will use, and explain why they are suitable for your research. Explain the scope of your research and describe the parameters clearly. Share your proposal with your supervisor and seek their feedback to refine your proposal.

f. Identifying supervisors

Identifying supervisors is essential to ensure that you have adequate support and guidance during your research project. Each institution might have

its own procedures in place and as a student, it is
your responsibility to check on these procedures.
Do not miss any briefing or orientation sessions
held for postgraduate students as these are the
sessions that will provide you with all information
related to procedures involved in your
postgraduate studies.

Here are some tips to help you identify your
supervisors. Identify researchers or faculty who
have published in your area of interest and have a
strong reputation in the field. Look at the
departmental website of your institution to identify
your supervisors who have similar research
interests. Speak to a few faculty members before
you decide on your supervisor.

Often, a reliable starting point will be the school or
center for postgraduate studies at your institution.
Speak to the officers in charge to gather some
information on the procedures in your institution
for the appointment of a supervisor. There could be
notification forms to be filled in and approvals to be
sought before your supervisor is confirmed.

Attending conferences and seminars related to your field to network with researchers and other postgraduate students is a good way to gather ideas for your proposal. Consult your peers and seniors to seek recommendations based on their experiences. Remember that finding the right supervisor is essential for the success of your postgraduate study. Choose a supervisor who has expertise in your field, is supportive, and has a mentoring approach that aligns with your working style.

It is important to note that upon working with a supervisor, avoid changing supervisors. As a postgraduate student, it is your right to change supervisors if you want but it would be a sheer waste of both your and your supervisor's time and effort each time you change supervisor. Each time you go to a new supervisor, you will have to restart engaging with the new supervisor and also it takes time to understand each other's work style. This will surely delay the completion of your studies. It is always advisable that you do your due diligence as a postgraduate student and identify the supervisor you want to work with till you complete your studies. So, identify your supervisors correctly based on the information you have gathered from the departments, your lecturers, and seniors who have completed their studies.

NOTES

Chapter 3

PLANNING AND MANAGING YOUR RESEARCH

Planning and managing your research involves a systematic approach to conducting research, from developing a research plan to executing the plan efficiently. It covers various aspects, such as defining research objectives, formulating research questions, selecting appropriate research methods, and selecting appropriate instruments. identifying data sources, and analyzing data.

Creating a research plan and work schedule helps in defining research objectives. A research plan helps in identifying the research objectives and outlining the scope of the study. It provides clarity and direction to the research process and ensures that the research stays focused and on track.

Further, well-planned research can save valuable time and resources by providing a roadmap for the research process. It helps to prioritize the research tasks and allocate time, effort, and resources efficiently. A research plan and work schedule help to facilitate communication and collaboration among team members. It ensures that everyone is on the same page and working towards the same goals. A well-planned and executed research increases the chances of success by reducing the likelihood of errors and ensuring that the research is rigorous and valid. Hence, consider the scope of your study and the financial implications to manage your resources.

Effective time management helps to prioritize tasks based on their importance and urgency. During the postgraduate journey, you will experience giving up on some of your favourite past-time commitments such as movies and hobbies. Consider these sacrifices as temporary and stay focussed on your goals. This focus also helps to avoid procrastination and ensures that critical tasks are completed on time. Effective time management reduces stress and anxiety by ensuring that deadlines are met, and tasks are completed on time. It helps to avoid last-minute rushes and ensures that the research process is less stressful. Effective time management increases productivity by enabling researchers to focus on the most important tasks and minimizing distractions. Preparing a Gantt chart to plan out your time helps in organising your study. Be cognizant that you want to complete your study within a few years.

Developing good research habits, such as being thorough, meticulous, and accurate ensures that the research is of high quality and meets the required standards. Good research habits increase efficiency by ensuring that the research process is well-organized, streamlined, and executed in a timely manner. Good research habits, such as being transparent, ethical, and honest, promote credibility and ensure that the research is trustworthy and reliable.

In conclusion, planning and managing your research, managing time effectively, and

Chapter 4

CONDUCTING YOUR RESEARCH

Conducting research and literature reviews, collecting and analyzing data, and using various research methodologies is a complex process that requires careful planning and execution.

Here is a general overview of the steps involved in this process:

1. Start by identifying a research problem and questions that you want to investigate. This will help you focus your research efforts and guide your literature review and data collection.

2. Conduct a comprehensive review of existing literature on your research topic to gain an understanding of the current state of knowledge, identify gaps in the literature, and develop a theoretical framework for your study.

3. Select a research methodology that is appropriate for your research question, data collection

methods, and data analysis techniques. Common research methodologies include qualitative, quantitative, and mixed methods approaches.

4. Create a research design that outlines the specific steps you will take to collect and analyze data. This should include a detailed description of your research question, research methods, data collection techniques, and data analysis methods.

5. Collect data using the methods outlined in your research design. This may involve conducting surveys, interviews, experiments, or other data collection techniques.

6. Analyze your data using appropriate statistical or qualitative analysis techniques. This will help you draw meaningful conclusions from your data and answer your research question.

7. Draw conclusions from your research findings and make recommendations based on your results. This will help you contribute to the existing body of knowledge and inform future research efforts.

8. Communicate your research findings through academic papers, presentations, or other means. This will help you disseminate your research and contribute to the larger academic community.

The radial Diagram 2 below summarises the above 8 steps:

Diagram 2: The Research Process

Overall, conducting research and literature reviews, collecting and analyzing data, and using various research methodologies is a complex process that requires careful planning and execution. By following these steps, you can ensure that your research is rigorous, valid, and contributes meaningfully to your field of study.

NOTES

Chapter 5

WRITING AND PRESENTING YOUR RESEARCH

Conducting research and literature reviews, collecting and analyzing data, and using various research methodologies is a complex process that requires careful planning and execution.

Here is a general overview of the steps involved in this process. Start by identifying a research question or problem that you want to investigate. This will help you focus your research efforts and guide your literature review and data collection.

First, conduct a comprehensive review of existing literature on your research topic to gain an understanding of the current state of knowledge, identify gaps in the literature, and develop a theoretical framework for your study. Then, select a research methodology that is appropriate for your research question, data collection methods, and data analysis techniques. Common research methodologies include qualitative, quantitative, and mixed methods approaches.

Next, create a research design that outlines the specific steps you will take to collect and analyze data. This should include a detailed description of your research question, research methods, data collection techniques, and data analysis methods. Collect data using the methods outlined in your research design. This may involve conducting surveys, interviews, experiments, or other data collection techniques.

Then, analyze your data using appropriate statistical or qualitative analysis techniques. This will help you draw meaningful conclusions from your data and answer your research question. Draw conclusions from your research findings and make recommendations based on your results. This will help you contribute to the existing body of knowledge and inform future research efforts. Communicate your research findings through academic papers, presentations, or other means. This will help you disseminate your research and contribute to the larger academic community. Overall, conducting research and literature reviews, collecting and analyzing data, and using various research methodologies is a complex process that requires careful planning and execution. By following these steps, you can ensure that your research is rigorous, valid, and contributes meaningfully to your field of study.

NOTES

Chapter 6

ETHICS AND INTEGRITY IN RESEARCH

Ethics refers to a set of moral principles and values that guide individuals and organizations on what is right and wrong, just and unjust, fair and unfair, and acceptable or unacceptable behaviour. Integrity, on the other hand, is the quality of being honest, trustworthy, and having strong moral principles.

In postgraduate research, ethics and integrity are essential because they ensure that researchers conduct their research in a responsible and ethical manner. This involves protecting the rights and welfare of human subjects, ensuring the safety, privacy and confidentiality of sensitive data, and maintaining scientific integrity and objectivity.

The importance of ethical research practices lies in the fact that research can have significant impacts on individuals, communities, and society as a whole. Therefore, researchers have a responsibility to ensure that their research is conducted in an ethical manner and that the benefits of the research outweigh any potential risks or harms.

Maintaining integrity throughout the research process involves adhering to ethical principles and guidelines, such as obtaining informed consent from study participants, ensuring the confidentiality and privacy of participants, disclosing conflicts of interest, avoiding plagiarism and other forms of research misconduct, ensuring the safety of data collected, and reporting research findings accurately and honestly.

To maintain ethical research practices, it is important for researchers to stay up-to-date on ethical guidelines and regulations in their field and to seek guidance from supervisors, colleagues, and institutional review boards as needed. It is also essential for researchers to maintain open and honest communication with study participants, colleagues, and stakeholders to ensure that their research is conducted in a transparent and accountable manner. Remember to get all consent in written form to refer to as evidence when the need arises.

NOTES

Chapter 7

SUPPORT SERVICES AND RESOURCES

Postgraduate research students have access to a variety of support services and resources, including academic and personal support. Here are some of the most common resources available to postgraduate research students at most institutions.

Postgraduate research students can access academic support services such as library resources, research methodology courses, writing support services, research workshops, and seminars. These services are designed to help postgraduate students develop the skills needed to conduct research and produce high-quality academic work.

Postgraduate research students will be assigned a research supervisor who will provide guidance and support throughout their research project. The research supervisor will provide feedback on the student's work and help them to refine their research questions, methodology, and writing.

Postgraduate research students may be eligible for scholarships or funding opportunities to support their research projects and publications. Students should check with their university or department to find out about available funding opportunities. This is important as most institutions include publications as core requirements for graduation. Many universities provide counselling services to support the mental health and well-being of their students. Postgraduate research students can access these services if they need support with issues such as stress, anxiety, or depression. I have observed that family commitment is one of the most common reasons for postgraduate students to withdraw from a programme. Hence, it's important that postgraduate students be guided on time management to ensure there's a healthy balance in their studies, work, and family lives.

Postgraduate research students with disabilities can access disability services to ensure that they have the necessary support to complete their research projects. These services may include access to assistive technology, modified course materials, and additional support from staff.

Postgraduate research students can access career services to help them prepare for their future careers. These services may include career counselling, job search support, and networking events.

Many universities have peer support groups for postgraduate research students. These groups provide an opportunity for students to connect with others who are going through similar experiences and to share tips and advice. Overall, postgraduate research students have access to a range of support services and resources to help them succeed in their research project and beyond.

Chapter 8

KEY TAKEAWAYS

This Handbook for Postgraduate Research Students provides valuable guidance and advice for students pursuing postgraduate research degrees.

Some key points that can be summarized from the handbook are:

- ❖ Postgraduate research is a challenging and rewarding experience that requires dedication, commitment, and a passion for the subject area.

Pursuing postgraduate research is an incredibly fulfilling and exciting experience, but it also requires a significant amount of hard work, dedication, and perseverance.

Postgraduate research involves delving deep into a specific area of study and conducting original research to advance knowledge and understanding in that field. This requires a high level of academic rigor and a commitment to conducting thorough and rigorous research.

In addition to academic skills, postgraduate research also requires strong organizational and time-management skills, as well as the ability to work independently and manage a complex research project. It's important for postgraduate researchers to be able to set goals, prioritize tasks, and manage their workload effectively.

Despite the challenges, postgraduate research can be an incredibly rewarding experience. It provides an opportunity to make a significant contribution to a field of study, develop expertise and skills that are highly valued by employers, and build valuable professional connections and networks.

Overall, postgraduate research is a challenging but incredibly rewarding experience for those who are passionate about their subject area and committed to pursuing knowledge and understanding at the highest level.

- ❖ Effective time management, organization, and communication skills are essential for success in postgraduate research.

Postgraduate research is a demanding process that requires a lot of time and effort. Effective time management is necessary to ensure that you are able to complete all your tasks within the given deadlines. This involves setting priorities, creating a schedule, and sticking to it. By managing your time effectively, you can avoid last-minute rushes, reduce stress, and maximize your productivity.

Postgraduate research involves managing a large amount of information, data, and resources. Effective organization skills are necessary to ensure that you can keep track of everything and access it when needed. This involves creating a system for storing and organizing your data, notes, and research materials. By staying organized, you can save time and avoid confusion.

Postgraduate research often involves working with other researchers, supervisors, and stakeholders. Effective communication skills are necessary to ensure that you can convey your ideas clearly, collaborate effectively, and present your research findings convincingly. This involves developing your written and oral communication skills, actively listening to feedback, and being open to different perspectives. By communicating effectively, you can build strong relationships, avoid misunderstandings, and enhance the impact of your research.

Overall, by developing strong time management, organization, and communication skills, you can improve your chances of success in postgraduate research and beyond.

❖ Building a supportive network of supervisors, peers, and other professionals can be invaluable for navigating the challenges of postgraduate research.

Undertaking research can be a challenging and often isolating experience, and having people around you who understand the research process and can offer guidance and support can make a big difference to your success.

Supervisors are often the first port of call for postgraduate researchers, and a good supervisor can provide valuable guidance and feedback throughout the research process. However, it's also important to build a network of peers and other professionals, as they can provide different perspectives, share their own experiences and insights, and offer support in different ways.

Peers can be a great source of support, both in terms of the emotional and practical aspects of research. Connecting with other researchers in your field can help you to feel less isolated and can provide a sense of community. You may also find that your peers can offer practical support, such as sharing resources or offering feedback on your work.

Other professionals can also be valuable members of your support network. For example, you may find it helpful to connect with librarians, who can provide guidance on literature searches and access to resources. You may also find it valuable to attend conferences or events where you can meet other professionals in your field, such as academics or industry experts.

Ultimately, building a supportive network can help you to navigate the challenges of postgraduate research more effectively, and can help you to achieve your goals. So don't be afraid to reach out to others and build those connections – you never know who might be able to offer the support and guidance you need.

❖ Students should take advantage of the various resources and opportunities available to them, including training and development programs, conferences, and funding opportunities.

These opportunities can help them develop new skills, gain knowledge, and build their professional network. Here are some reasons why students should take advantage of these resources.

Training and development programs are designed to enhance students' skills in various areas such as communication, leadership, problem-solving, and critical thinking. These skills are highly valued by employers and can help students stand out in the job market.

Attending conferences and events is an excellent way for students to meet professionals in their field and build their network. These connections can be beneficial for finding internships, job opportunities, and mentorship.

There are numerous funding opportunities available for students, including scholarships, grants, and awards. These can help students cover the cost of tuition, travel, research expenses, and other educational costs.

In conclusion, taking advantage of the various resources and opportunities available to students can have numerous benefits. It can help them develop new skills, expand their network, and fund their education. Therefore, it's important for students to research and explore these opportunities and make the most of them.

- ❖ It is essential to maintain a healthy work-life balance and prioritize self-care to avoid burnout and maintain motivation.

When individuals prioritize self-care and balance their work and personal lives, they can reduce stress, increase motivation and productivity, and improve their overall quality of life.

Working long hours, neglecting personal relationships, and failing to engage in self-care activities can lead to burnout, which can have significant negative consequences for both physical and mental health. Burnout can lead to physical symptoms like fatigue, headaches, and gastrointestinal problems, as well as mental health issues like depression and anxiety.

To maintain a healthy work-life balance, individuals can take steps such as setting clear boundaries between work and personal time, prioritizing self-care activities like exercise, meditation, and hobbies, and practicing effective time management strategies. It's also important to maintain healthy relationships with loved ones and to seek support when necessary, whether from friends, family, or mental health professionals.

Prioritizing self-care and maintaining a healthy work-life balance is crucial for avoiding burnout, reducing stress, and improving overall well-being. It is important to recognize that self-care is not selfish but is an essential part of taking care of oneself and being able to perform at work and in personal life to the best of one's abilities.

This Handbook for Postgraduate Research Students provides students with a comprehensive guide that can help them successfully navigate the postgraduate research journey and achieve their academic and professional goals.

In conclusion, postgraduate research is an exciting and challenging journey that requires a range of skills and support. This Handbook for Postgraduate Research Students provides valuable guidance and advice, but students should also seek out additional support and guidance as needed from their supervisors, peers, and other professionals. By leveraging the resources and opportunities available to them and prioritizing their well-being, postgraduate research students can achieve their goals and make meaningful contributions to their field of study.

NOTES

Chapter 9

CONCLUSION

Reading various guidelines and tips shared by experienced researchers is one sure way to prepare oneself mentally and psychologically before embarking on a postgraduate programme. Understanding the research process thoroughly will pave a smoother pathway to completion of the study. Often, students dive into a postgraduate programme without understanding the research process.

Remember to read widely to identify the research problem. So, most often literature review precedes identifying the problem. Accept the fact that doing research is a complex process and expecting a linear progress in your research can lead to frustration. As much as planning is critical in research but your plan will evolve as you progress and this flexibility and fluidity must be expected and supported throughout the research process.

The norm in research is to go back and forth in your writing to ensure there is cohesion and coherence in presenting data and findings.

It is my earnest hope that with this handbook as a guide postgraduate students will have a manageable academic journey to successfully complete their studies. There is no quick way or easy solution to accomplishing postgraduate qualifications, especially in research-based programmes.

With steel determination and consistent hard work, students will be able to head towards success confidently. The guidelines provided in this handbook are intended to guide the students through the arduous postgraduate journey and are not meant to be a quick fix to achieving postgraduate academic qualifications.

Research Matrix

No.	Article Citation	Approach/ Design	Site/ Sample	Objectives	RQs	Findings	Future Research
1.							
2.							
3.							
4.							
5.							
6.							

Appendix B

Sample Gantt Chart

Year	**1**		**2**		**3**		**NOTES**
Semester	**1**	**2**	**1**	**2**	**1**	**2**	
Month	**Sept**	**Jan**	**Sept**	**Jan**	**Sept**	**Jan**	
Proposal							
Defence							
Data Collection							
Data Analysis							
Final Writeup							
Viva							

www.ingramcontent.com/pod-product-compliance
Lightning Source LLC
Chambersburg PA
CBHW050655250726
48662CB00002B/692